Original title:
Succulent Silence

Copyright © 2025 Creative Arts Management OÜ
All rights reserved.

Author: Gabriel Kingsley
ISBN HARDBACK: 978-1-80581-814-4
ISBN PAPERBACK: 978-1-80581-341-5
ISBN EBOOK: 978-1-80581-814-4

Murmurs of the Unheard

In a room where no one talks,
A cat sneezes, everyone mocks.
The ticking clock, it taps away,
Boredom's game is here to play.

With silent snickers, we conspire,
A ghostly giggle takes us higher.
We mime our laughs like children's pranks,
Imagining all the silent ranks.

The Weight of a Whisper

A little bird's chirp, then it stops,
As if it thinks: 'That's how it flops!'
We all lean in, ears like radar,
Hoping for secrets, bizarre and afar!

But silence weighs in, thick as honey,
Where jokes are buried, cold but funny.
Laughter in our heads, like an exercise,
Trading winks while rolling our eyes.

Hidden Treasures of Tranquil Times

Between the giggles and stifled snorts,
Are treasures hidden in quiet reports.
Each silence is a treasure chest,
Full of jokes that playfully jest.

The art of shushing while we burst,
To hold the laughter feels like a curse.
In silence, we unleash our cheer,
A whisper laughed, oh, what a sneer!

A Dance Without Sound

They twirl and sway with no ballad to sing,
Each move a giggle, what joy they bring.
A dance in the void, a sight to behold,
As laughter tiptoes, hearts unfold.

Feet shuffle close, with no rhythm to heed,
Yet joy's the language, we all can read.
With gestures grand, we paint the air,
Mimicking the quiet with flair and care.

Hues of Hushed Affection

In whispers soft and light,
A bubble pops, a cat takes flight.
Tea spills like secrets on the floor,
Giggles dance behind the door.

The clock ticks slow, it yawns, it grins,
As shadows play their silly sins.
A wink, a nod, a crafty cheer,
The blender hums a waltz so near.

Beneath the Quiet Canopy

Underneath the leafy hugs,
A squirrel pirouettes, it shrugs.
Chirps and chuckles fill the air,
While frogs attempt their two-step flair.

A picnic spread, mishaps abound,
The ants conspire without a sound.
Lemonade drips, a rogue mosquito,
Yet laughter blooms, oh what a show!

A Brocade of Breath

In moments silken, mischief roams,
A sneeze erupts, alas, it foams.
Pancakes stack up, wobbling high,
As syrup flows, our spirits fly.

The gentle hush holds comical tales,
Of socks that vanish, and beefy snails.
With each small laugh, the world feels bright,
In our quiet space, joy takes flight.

The Serene Interlude

In stillness wrapped around a chair,
A goldfish swims, with nary a care.
My phone goes off, it's still on mute,
The dog's confused, but he's quite cute.

Soft chuckles rise like mist at dawn,
A note falls down, and yawns are drawn.
The world outside may rush and race,
But here we giggle at our own pace.

Still Waters Run Deep

In the pond, a frog sings loud,
Hoping to impress the passing crowd.
But the fish just roll their eyes,
While the dragonfly quietly sighs.

A turtle takes a lazy dive,
Claiming it's the best way to thrive.
But all the fish just giggle and float,
As the turtle tries hard not to gloat.

Ripe Thickets of Rest

In the bushes, a squirrel is bold,
Gathering acorns, a sight to behold.
He trips on a twig, goes tumbling down,
With a thud that could silence a clown.

The bunnies nearby start to cheer,
As the squirrel shakes off his fear.
"I meant to do that!" he claims with glee,
While the leaves just whisper, "Let it be."

Blossoms of Peace

A flower blooms in the bright sunlight,
Swatting away bugs with all its might.
Its petals dance and twirl with flair,
While bees buzz in a frantic, wild scare.

The sunflowers laugh, standing tall and proud,
As the dainty little flower attracts a crowd.
But one bee trips and falls on its face,
Creating an uproar that fills the space.

Echoes of the Heart

A heart once whispered a silly joke,
But the laughter came from a nearby oak.
It chuckled so hard, it wobbled left,
Creating echoes that felt quite deft.

The moon rolled his eyes at the duo's fun,
While stars blinked in laughter, one by one.
In this quiet space, jokes take their flight,
Crafting a night that feels just right.

Threads of Muffled Sound

In a room filled with whispers,
I tiptoe on air,
Missing the chance,
To laugh at a chair.

The cat gives me side-eye,
Like she knows my plan,
But I'm too busy giggling,
At my invisible fan.

The clock ticks away,
In its loudest disguise,
Counting the moments
Of my silent surprise.

My socks make a statement,
With colors so bright,
Yet my thoughts are all muted,
In this hilarious light.

Embracing the Soft Echo

In a world of soft murmurs,
Laughter often strays,
I mimic my echo,
As it joins in my plays.

A banana slipped past me,
In a dance of delight,
Fruits on the floor plotting,
To join in the night.

I hear giggles from shadows,
As the chairs shake and sway,
Could it be my grandpa?
Or just a joke on display?

Caught in a whirlwind,
Of banter unseen,
Each joke drops like confetti,
In this silent routine.

Where the Quiet Blooms

In a garden of whispers,
A flower starts to yawn,
Its petals are chuckling,
At the sight of the dawn.

The bees are on strike,
To find their buzzing flair,
But I spot them all snickering,
As they float in the air.

I chat with the daisies,
They giggle in glee,
As I trip over roots,
Like a root-bound bumblebee.

This hush truly hums,
With the blooms in the breeze,
Where the laughter of silence
Can tickle the trees.

The Poetry of Absence

In a store without sound,
I find a lost shoe,
Whispering sweet nothings,
To a sandwich or two.

The ghost of a donut,
Flew by with a wink,
Its frosting still swirling,
As I stop there to think.

I mumble to cupcakes,
With frosting so bold,
Their sprinkles just giggle,
While I wander and scold.

In absence, there's laughter,
In space, there's a jest,
Where the sights of the feast,
Will always be best.

Whispers of Velvet Tranquility

In a garden where giggles lie,
The flowers smile as bees float by.
They dance on petals, what a sight!
Even the grass is ticklish tonight.

Clouds drift past like cotton candy,
Birds tweet gossip, oh so dandy.
A breeze sneezes, the leaves all shake,
Nature's joke, don't make a mistake!

Squirrels prance with acorn hats,
Rabbits laugh at silly chats.
Beneath the moon's playful glance,
Even shadows join the dance.

Laughter bubbles from the stream,
Wishing wells share a secret dream.
In this stillness, fun is crowned,
A quiet joy, truly profound.

The Soft Embrace of Stillness

In corners where soft cushions hug,
A turtle hums a fuzzy drug.
Resting mice in blankets curled,
This is how sleepy dreams are twirled.

Whiskers twitch as night owls joke,
Teacups clink where the foxes smoke.
A cat yawns wide, showing its grin,
Even the stars let laughter in.

Leaves giggle in the gentle breeze,
While snails race slow, if you please.
Pillowed clouds in a slumber deep,
Who knew stillness could be this cheap?

Echoes whisper, tickling our ears,
In the silence, joy appears.
Soft embraces hold us tight,
In this calm, everything feels right.

Lush Echoes in the Quiet

Beneath the foliage, bubbles float,
A frog turns singer, taking notes.
In the quiet, there's a band,
With whispers, jokes, oh so grand!

Mushrooms giggle in their spots,
The sun's rays peek, tying knots.
A sloth strums its leafy guitar,
While crickets chirp, they're bizarre!

The breeze pulls pranks with feathered friends,
Tickling tails, making amends.
In this stillness, a world so bright,
Even shadows seem to delight.

Giggly roots reach for the sun,
In this lush silence, all is fun.
Nature winks, what a surprise,
Echoes of laughter in disguise.

Serene Gardens of Unspoken Dreams

In a patch where whispers bloom,
Stars are shy to share their tune.
Moths flutter in their tiny choir,
While daisies blush, oh so inspired.

In the hush, a turtle makes a stand,
Sporting shades and a cool band.
The garden gnomes start their debate,
Who gardens better? It's first-rate!

Crickets play the nighttime game,
Boredom's just not in their name.
Even the ants are plotting schemes,
In serene gardens of muted dreams.

Flowers wink, their petals sway,
As night wraps up the playful day.
Within this hush, laughter gleams,
Unspoken joy in vibrant themes.

Silence Cradled in Grass

In a patch of soft green grass,
Lies a rabbit, quite the sass.
Whispers bounce, no need to shout,
While the world spins, there's no doubt.

The ants march on in careful lines,
Holding tiny, grand designs.
A grasshopper makes a joyful leap,
Quiet as a secret we keep.

Dandelions dance in the breeze,
While frogs croak with such expertise.
The wind cracks jokes, but no one hears,
Just nature's laughter through the years.

Beneath the sun, everything chill,
Even the chill gets a thrill.
In this hush, the fun's alive,
In the silence, all things thrive.

Unfolding in Tranquil Air

Clouds drift like marshmallows sweet,
While squirrels chase with speedy feet.
A gentle sigh slips through the trees,
Where laughter rides the playful breeze.

The flowers smirk, their colors bright,
As the sun plays peek-a-boo light.
Butterflies flit with silly grace,
Each landing is a clumsy race.

Bubbles dance from a nearby brook,
A fish glances up, gives a look.
It seems the world forgot to frown,
In this canvas, joy is found.

Under the sky, a hidden glee,
In stillness, there's a mischief spree.
Embracing quiet, hearts take flight,
In laughter wrapped, all feels just right.

Serenity's Embrace

A cat snores loud on a sunny spot,
While shadows play, twist, and knot.
Pigeons strut with an air of pride,
As dogs roll over, far and wide.

The leaves gossip in perfect turns,
While the world spins and laughter churns.
A turtle moves slow, as if to tease,
In this peace, time finds its ease.

A breeze blows softly, hair askew,
With whispers of mischief, it breezes through.
The sun winks down on a wandering thought,
In tranquil moments, we find what we've sought.

Each quiet chuckle, a secret shared,
In laughter's echo, no one is scared.
In the warmth of soft, playful space,
Life is a jest, wrapped in grace.

The Gift of Absence

In the space where chatter fled,
Geraniums giggle instead.
Whispers dance on empty chairs,
Even the cat pretends and stares.

A cactus in a corner muses,
On jokes that no one ever chooses.
The clock ticks with a silly grin,
'What's time if no one's home to spin?'

A silence bloomed like brick-walled fun,
With no one here, it weighs a ton.
Yet in this hush, my thoughts run wild,
Like a puppy lost, or a hyper child.

So here's to missing all the noise,
To tranquil moments and quiet joys.
Who knew absence could be such a treat?
Like ice cream cones or dancing feet!

Meadow of Muffled Memories

In a field where echoes lay still,
I planted laughter, watered with will.
Each blade of grass a tickled tale,
Uproarious giggles ride the gale.

The daisies nod in muted cheer,
'We miss the ruckus, bring back the peers!'
Yet, they sway with a cheeky smile,
Playing hide and seek with silence awhile.

A butterfly whispers its woven plot,
"Was that a pun? Or just forgot?"
While clouds above pull off a prank,
Turning sunshine sharply to blank.

This meadow thrives in quiet cheer,
With whispers wild, drawing near.
In every pause, a giggle hides,
Amongst the flowers, slapstick glides!

Tapestry of Still Moments

In threads of quiet, colors blend,
They weave a tale where jesters send.
A lullaby that jumps in place,
With each still moment leaving a trace.

The canvas yawns with sleepy fun,
As time dribbles like a melted bun.
A painting done in muffled hues,
Where laughter tucks itself in snooze.

The yarns spin tales, absurd and bright,
Of socks that lost their partner's fight.
Each knot a giggle, neatly sewn,
In silence, humor's seeds are grown.

So let's toast to this woven cheer,
In stillness, find what we hold dear.
For laughter lives in subtle strokes,
A tapestry of silly jokes!

Silence Wrapped in Velvet

Cocooned in calm, where whispers hide,
I tiptoe softly, a giggling guide.
In velvet folds, the chuckles creep,
Hilarious thoughts that peek and leap.

Like marshmallows dressed in sweet regret,
Silence blooms, a cunning pet.
It's a plush embrace, a muffled roar,
Where every laugh's a secret door.

A squirrel scampers in muted glee,
Hoarding jokes like nuts in a tree.
Paradise found in hushed delight,
Undercover humor takes to flight.

So when stillness wraps around your day,
Remember to let that laughter play.
For in silence, joy might just take
A velvet ride, no need to fake!

The Gentle Breath of Peace

In a corner where stillness sprawls,
A cat snoozes, dreaming of fishy halls.
The clock ticks softly on the wall,
Time slips by, like a doughnut's fall.

A creaky chair rocks with glee,
Whispers of snacks, come sit with me.
A tumbleweed rolls past the grass,
While I sip my tea and watch the sass.

Hushed Sighs Beneath the Moon

Beneath the glow of a giddy moon,
Crickets hum a lazy tune.
A raccoon sneaks a midnight snack,
While stars giggle, 'Oh, look at that!'

The owl hoots with a comical flair,
As shadows dance without a care.
In this silence, laughter bloom,
As nature's jesters claim the room.

Solitude's Tender Shade

A lone bench sits in a leafy park,
Two squirrels dance in a nutty spark.
The breeze whispers jokes to the trees,
While dandelions float with ease.

A lonely bench, with bread as bait,
Nearby pigeons flock, oh what a fate!
They squawk and chatter, a feathered crowd,
For crumbs of wisdom, they're all too proud.

The Lullaby of Nature's Palette

Colors swirl in the soft daylight,
Butterflies laugh at a flower's fright.
Painted skies play tricks on the eyes,
While bees buzz tales in sweet disguise.

Even the rocks seem to chuckle and grin,
As worms do cartwheels beneath their skin.
In this calm, where humor's laid bare,
Nature's art brings us laughter to share.

Blossoming in the Stillness

In the garden where whispers sprout,
Giggles hide without a doubt.
Petals laugh in colors bright,
While bees buzz softly, not in fright.

Laughter hides beneath the leaves,
Stumbling on unspoken thieves.
A snail slips on a punchline true,
Who knew slowness could be so blue?

Bunnies hop with silent cheer,
Their ears perked up, they disappear.
A dance of winks and quiet grins,
The hush unfolds where the fun begins.

In this hush, the jokes conspire,
With every pause, increasing fire.
Who needs noise when giggles bloom?
In silence, joy finds every room.

Enigma of the Unvoiced

Words have fled, but humor lingers,
Tickled toes and dancing fingers.
A shrug, a grin, the secret's shared,
In unvoiced tales, laughter's bared.

The clock ticks slow, each second's game,
With silent snickers, who's to blame?
Invisible gags just fill the air,
Like cats that plot without a care.

Rabbits wink, they plot and scheme,
In the quiet, they chase a dream.
Whispers curl like smoke in the sun,
In the stillness, they have their fun.

A nod, a glance, conspiratorial,
Each moment grand and historical.
Soliloquies dance on muted winds,
This silent jest—where laughter begins.

The Joy of Emptiness

In empty spaces, joy is found,
With quiet chuckles all around.
An echo dashes off a wall,
Bounces back to start a brawl.

A vacant chair, a lively jest,
A bear who thinks he's dressed the best.
No noise to drown the snorts so sweet,
As giggling shadows skip down the street.

Where silence brews, the bubbling fun,
Ideas float like clouds on the run.
A squirrel sneezes, and the world erupts,
In this hush, the silliness erupts.

Nothing's worse than a quiet space,
Where laughter hides behind a face.
In emptiness, there's room to play,
Like socks that tie and run away!

Sanctuary of Soft Echoes

In a room where echoes softly tread,
Socks in the corner, smiles widespread.
A cactus dreams of spaghetti nights,
While crickets provide the silly sights.

Wobbling chairs dance a funky beat,
As dust bunnies get up on their feet.
A tickle trapped in the stillness hums,
Waiting for giggles from tiny drums.

Ears perk up at the foam of glee,
When silence sways effortlessly.
Each squeak a burst, each hush a tease,
Whispers strut with grand unease.

In echoes soft, the fun finds way,
Turning every pause into a play.
Where silence reigns, let laughter burst,
In the sanctuary, the joy immerses.

Serenity Wrapped in Silence

In the hush of a nap, cats dream of fish,
A sneeze in the stillness, oh what a wish.
While the goldfish just glares, unaware of the plight,
As the world softly chuckles at this silent delight.

Bubbles from soda lightly fill up the air,
A whisper of laughter tumbles everywhere.
The quiet is loud, like a tickling tick,
Where silence and giggles waltz, oh so slick.

Jellybeans roll on the table in rows,
The sound of a chair creaks and everyone knows.
Even the spoons in the drawer start to play,
As they sing to the forks in a comical way.

So let's toast to the moments where noise takes a break,
And laughter is hidden in each silly mistake.
In the peace of a pause, life adds a surprise,
As we giggle in stillness, oh my, what a prize!

Quietude's Enchanted Hideaway

In a drowsy old cottage with creaky old floors,
The mice waltz around on their cozy little tours.
A teacup is giggling, it's filled to the brim,
While the biscuits are plotting a sly little whim.

Outside, the trees whisper secrets to bees,
Who buzz with delight under soft, gentle breeze.
While a frog on a lily pad sings jazz so sweet,
As the dragonflies tap and bounce to the beat.

A cat in a hat reads a book upside down,
While a peacock struts proudly in a feathered crown.
All the quiet is tangled in stories so bright,
Where laughter and silliness light up the night.

So come take a stroll through this dreamy abode,
Where giggles and chuckles are freely bestowed.
In the hush, you'll find whispers of fun all around,
With the magic of quiet, let joy be unbound!

The Secret Language of Stillness

When time takes a pause, the clock starts to snore,
And the toaster hums softly as bread starts its chore.
The curtains might giggle, the shadows might dance,
As a chair takes a leap in a bold, silly prance.

In the stillness of twilight, the crickets all chat,
Sharing tall tales while wearing a hat.
The silence is filled with the silliest sighs,
As the world spins around in an unexpected surprise.

A slumbering snail dreams of racing grand mice,
While the flowers all whisper, 'We're quiet, be nice!'
A breeze starts to chuckle and shakes all the trees,
Throwing leaves in a flutter, as if tickled by bees.

In the calm, there's a murmur, a jest or a jest,
Where stillness is wild, and nothing can rest.
So lean in, dear friend, and sip on this brew,
Of laughter wrapped in quiet, just waiting for you!

Tranquil Blooming in the Heart

In a garden of whispers, where daisies reside,
The pencils are doodling, taking the ride.
A little bird giggles while twirling in glee,
Sipping dew drops like tea from the leaf of a tree.

When shadows grow long and the sun winks its eye,
The butterflies gossip and flutter on by.
A snail in a turtleneck, fashionably late,
Ponders life's riddles, while balancing fate.

Under the moon's smirk, the daisies all buzz,
Talking of secrets that quietness does.
Each petal a story, a joke wrapped in cheer,
In the bloom of our hearts, let silliness steer.

So linger awhile, in this tranquil domain,
Where laughter blooms freely, dissolving the pain.
In the softest of moments, find joy with a twist,
As silence wraps laughter in a sweet little mist!

A Pause in the Wind

A squirrel snickers at a tree,
Why do birds chirp so happily?
The breeze just sits, it takes a break,
While ants engage in a funny shake.

A leaf flies by, doing a dance,
It twirls around without a chance.
A cat looks up, tilts its head,
What's that? Just wind, that's what I said.

The clouds drift in a lazy way,
While sprinkles decide to join the play.
A snail slowly grins, feeling proud,
It's the king of this empty crowd.

In this calm, the laughter's near,
Nature plays jokes that we all hear.
Pause with me, in this light spin,
Joy is found when silence begins.

Savoring the Void

A muffin laughs, with crumbs that fall,
'What's the joke?' it says to all.
Space is big, yet here we sit,
In this quiet, we find some wit.

The clock ticks loud, with such a tease,
It slows down just to see us freeze.
A butterfly flaps, but it's a bore,
When no one's around to watch it soar.

I spilled some tea, it made a splash,
The cats just purr, and laugh at the crash.
In this stillness, shenanigans brew,
As nothing much is going to do.

So let's toast to the empty air,
With giggles popping everywhere.
In silence, the fun starts to unfold,
In the void, pure joy we behold.

The Beauty of a Silent Moment

An empty chair sits with style,
It beckons me to pause a while.
A dust mote dances in the sun,
Is it alone? No, it has fun!

The microphone left on its stand,
Whispers tales of a band unplanned.
A squirrel yawns and gives a stretch,
In silent moments, life's a sketch.

The toaster laughs—its slots are bare,
What's breakfast without a little care?
The kitchen holds its breath in glee,
As smells arise from longing tea.

Here's to silence, thick and round,
In it, the sweetest laughs are found.
A moment shared, a chuckle's charm,
In quiet, all things disarm.

Lush Serenity

A frog in a pond, staring wide,
Wondering where all the flies have dried.
With no one to croak a witty line,
It ponders hard if life's a sign.

The flowers giggle, petal to petal,
As bees just buzz and dream of metal.
The grass whispers secrets to the breeze,
It's a comedy show with no one to please.

Overhead, the sky wears a grin,
Clouds play tag, oh where've they been?
In the quiet, they tickle the day,
While shadows laugh in a sneaky way.

With each chuckle that passes by,
In this green, a soft lullaby.
So let's savor the peace and cheer,
In lush serenity, humor is near.

Echoes in the Emptiness

In a room full of echoes, I try not to sneeze,
My cat gives a glance, she just wants some cheese.
I talk to the curtains, they flutter and sway,
Whispering secrets they hear day by day.

The chair wants to gossip, it creaks in delight,
But all I can hear is the clock's tick tonight.
A sock on the floor wears a very sad frown,
It's tired of being the lone sock in town.

Floating with thoughts, they bounce off the wall,
The fridge has a riddle, but it won't share at all.
A dance with my shadow that keeps tripping me,
It giggles and twirls, as happy as can be!

In this vast empty space, we put on our show,
A comedy act with no audience to know.
Though quiet surrounds me, the laughs stay awhile,
In echoes of silence, I find a sweet smile.

Softness of Solitude

The couch throws a party, with pillows to spare,
Popcorn on the table begins to declare:
'Join in on the fun, we're quiet and free!'
I sit with my thoughts and sip herbal tea.

My socks start a journey, they dance on the floor,
They spin and they sway, oh, what's in store?
The dust bunnies giggle, they roll with delight,
In the glow of the lamp, everything feels right.

Outside there's a bird, who thinks it can chat,
But all that I hear is a vague kind of spat.
So I smile at the stillness, with a chuckle or two,
Softness surrounds me, like a warm, cozy shoe.

In this realm of quiet, where laughter is soft,
The world spins around me, but I'm aloft.
With whispers of giggles and a wink from the chair,
Softness of solitude—the perfect affair.

Gardens of Tranquility

In gardens of calm where the gnomes have a say,
They water the flowers, then nap through the day.
A snail takes its time, with a pace like a hug,
While crickets throw tea parties, all snug as a bug.

A breeze swirls about, tickling leaves on the trees,
It's like nature's laughter, a symphony of tease.
The daisies look up, and they wink with a smile,
While the roses recite poetry, free for a while.

I plop down on a bench, hold a snack in my hand,
Birds squawk in approval, like they understand.
With a chuckle, I ponder, who's gardener here?
The pumpkins are plotting a pie-making sphere!

In this tranquil garden, all senses awake,
Every rustle and whisper, a delightful mistake.
A laugh in this space brings peace to the air,
In gardens of stillness, we dance without care.

Hushed Reverie

In the corners of stillness, my mind starts to play,
With thoughts that are lofty, then tumble away.
Pillow fights with shadows, they tremble and roll,
While daydreams throw parties inside of my soul.

With a sip of my coffee, it froths in delight,
The mug gives a wink, wishing me a good night.
The silence, it chuckles, in whispers it twirls,
As a sock puppet master juggles my swirls.

I find a delight in the tick-tock parade,
Where time takes a breather, all worries then fade.
And the cat in her napping, seems lost in a dream,
While the furniture plans an escape from the beam.

In hushed reveries where the laughter is slight,
I bloom with the quiet, feeling ever so bright.
With every small giggle that dances the air,
In the hush of the moment, I find we're a pair.

Beneath the Quiet Sky

Beneath the sky, so still and blue,
The squirrels complain, who knew?
Birds gossip softly, sharing a joke,
While the breeze giggles and gives a poke.

With whispers fluttering near the ground,
A cat in the shade, less dignified, found.
She spies a fly, her eyes in a whirl,
Then misshapes her leap, what a tumble and twirl!

The flowers snicker, petals in glee,
As a snail slides by, perhaps with a plea.
"Don't rush!" it shouts, "Life's sweet as pie!"
But who's to listen, when all else is shy?

In the playful hush, a tickle of time,
A giggle escapes, like a nursery rhyme.
Beneath this calm, laughter can sway,
In the stillness, silliness stays!

Chasing the Sighs

In a world where whispers zoom,
And giggles quiver in every room,
We chase the sighs that dance in the air,
Tickled by silence, laughter laid bare.

A turtle makes plans, oh what a grand feat,
To outpace a breeze, isn't that sweet?
He takes off slow, with a grin on his face,
It's the lightest of races, in this funny space.

Clouds bump together, drifting in cheer,
While raindrops snatch giggles from here to there.
"Did you hear that?" a moonbeam will say,
"It's only the giggles of night slipping away!"

In the stillness, we linger and jest,
Though no one knows this place could be a fest.
So we chase the sighs, a game so absurd,
In the hush of the night, we simply concur.

The Gentle Lullaby

The moon winks softly, humming a tune,
While stars can't help but laugh and swoon.
A gentle lullaby plays in the night,
Cherubs chuckle, holding their light.

A bear in a hammock tries to nap,
But his dreams are tangled, what a mishap!
He wanders through fields of marshmallow pies,
In the quiet, he finds funny surprise.

With crickets chirping their offbeat song,
A soft breeze clarifies thoughts that are wrong.
"Did you hear that?" asks a leaf with a grin,
As giggles escape where the joy can begin.

In this airy space where whimsy takes flight,
We'll dance together till the end of the night.
A lullaby wraps each echoing thought,
Where laughter and peace are all that we've sought.

Reverie in Soft Shadows

In shadows that sway, a dream giggles on,
With a flicker of light just before dawn.
A gopher with glasses reads a small book,
Laughing at life with a wise little look.

Whispers cross paths like silly old friends,
Where kittens plot mischief that never quite ends.
They tumble, they slide, all in the hush,
While the trees hum along without any rush.

A firefly twinkles, the night's little star,
Joking with crickets from near and afar.
As bats take their flight with style and grace,
We giggle and chuckle in this shadowy space.

In reveries soft, we find our delight,
With laughter and fun, each moment feels right.
In a world full of calm, where silliness glows,
We dance in the shadows, just letting it flow!

The Language of Quietude

Whispers dance on the breeze,
As squirrels gossip with trees.
A snail slides by, quite a sight,
In the hush, he takes flight.

The birds forget their grand tunes,
Chasing shadows and balloons.
With fingers crossed and toes too,
They giggle beneath the sky so blue.

In corners, the crickets conspire,
With echoes that never tire.
Each silence speaks a loud joke,
While the cat is left to poke.

So let the quiet reign high,
With puns the owls can't deny.
In this world of funny still,
Even silence has its thrill.

Reflection in Still Waters

The pond reflects a clownish face,
In ripples that dance with grace.
Frogs hold court on lily pads,
While turtles dodge their quiet jabs.

A fish splashes in dismay,
Did it snag the wrong cliché?
With every plop and plunk of grace,
Deep wisdom laughs in the same place.

Reflections twirl and twist around,
The news of the day's absurd found.
Like water's wink that won't stay still,
The fun floats by with gentle thrill.

So gaze upon the shimmering show,
Where silence hums a vibrant glow.
Beneath the calm, the chuckles rise,
In each soft ripple, laughter lies.

Soft Shadows of the Heart

In shadows where giggles creep,
The heart wears chuckles, not deep.
Little whispers, like soft rain,
Bring joy and tease the mundane.

A tickle here, a nudge there,
Finding joy in the empty air.
Like shadows casting humorous sighs,
Surprises in where quiet lies.

With every pause, a jest is made,
In stillness, the laughter's laid.
The heart's rhythm beats a tune,
Do we dance in silence or swoon?

So listen close, let laughter blend,
In stillness, each joke is a friend.
For in shadows where silence plays,
The heart giggles in secret ways.

When Time Stands Still

The clock ticks in a lazy sway,
While cats nap the hours away.
A mime is trapped in a glass case,
Mocking time with a silly face.

Every second bends and teases,
Like boogers that dance in breezes.
In moments hushed, the comical thrives,
As patience kills, but laughter drives.

With silence rimming the air,
Balloons float without a care.
The world wraps in a cozy hug,
Where even stillness gives a shrug.

So let the moment tease and thrill,
Where time is but a playful quill.
In quiet hours, find the fun,
For laughter blossoms with the sun.

Gentle Secrets

Whispers float on ladybug wings,
Dandelion puffs and hidden things.
Muffled giggles in cozy nooks,
A cat's sly grin, and lazy books.

Cereal crunch in a still-lit room,
Cartoon reruns chase away gloom.
The clock ticks soft, a gentle tease,
Time's playful jest, if you please.

Smiles exchanged without a word,
A breeze that dances, unheard,
Jelly beans tossed in a fun race,
Laughter erupts, a warm embrace.

In this garden of quiet cheer,
Every giggle is crystal clear.
We bloom in harmony, wild and free,
Secrets shared, just you and me.

Unspoken Depths

In the pond, a frog does leap,
Ripples sound like secrets keep.
An otter sneaks in for a snack,
Dreams run free, no need to track.

A sturdy boat floats near the shore,
Sailing on waves, but wanting more.
Giggles burst like popcorn's pop,
On this serene yet silly stop.

Bubbles rise, they giggle too,
Each one forms a joke or two.
Banana peels on nature's floor,
Laughing with the trees galore.

In quiet, what fun things unfold,
Adventures spark as we grow old.
Unspoken depths of joy delight,
In giggles bright, we take flight.

Vibrations of Peace

Crisp apples crunch as laughter sings,
The cat sprawls out, queen of kings.
Sunbeams chuckle, in colors bright,
Dancing through day into the night.

Kittens tumble in soft delight,
Previously perched in peaceful sight.
The fridge hums a mellow tune,
It's a symphony, morning to noon.

Serenade of fluttering leaves,
There lies joy in what deceives.
A whisper shared by clouds above,
Wiggles of peace, a gentle shove.

As clockworks click, the world feels light,
Funny how stillness ignites.
In this calm, hearts run amok,
Peaceful vibes in the laugh of a clock.

Sheltered From Noise

Under blankets, giggles thrive,
Muffled whispers keep us alive.
Cookies crunched in whispered glee,
The loudest secret, just you and me.

Beneath the roof, the world fades away,
Socks in mismatched colors play.
A sneaky cat on the table jumps,
In all this chaos, we hide our humps.

Lollipop dreams and days of bliss,
Unlock the giggles we can't miss.
With each smile, the candles glow,
A sweet retreat as life flows slow.

Cuddled tight away from sound,
In our shelter, silliness is found.
Who knew quiet could be so loud?
A quiet laugh, then we're so proud.

Nature's Embrace of Stillness

In the woods where squirrels nap,
And the bees forgot to flap,
A turtle wears a crown of grass,
Wondering why the world won't pass.

Trees gossip in rustling leaves,
Making jokes of silly thieves.
The flowers giggle, soft and bright,
As crickets dance in pure delight.

The Peaceful Breath of Dusk.

The sun yawns with a sleepy grin,
While shadows gather, pulling in.
A cat plots mischief, takes a seat,
Declaring evening's calm retreat.

Fireflies waltz with lazy grace,
As hedgehogs comically embrace.
The moon plays hide and seek with stars,
While frogs serenade from afar.

Whispers of Stillness

In the garden, things stand still,
Until a snail insists on thrill.
A rooster fails to wake the dawn,
And the daisies just move on.

Laziness hums in the air,
As hedgehogs play a game of dare.
The wind sits down to have a chat,
While a hedgehog wears a silly hat.

The Quiet Harvest

In fields where silent laughter grows,
Pumpkins chuckle in autumn's clothes.
Corn keeps secrets, tall and shy,
As bees pretend to be a fly.

Carrots whisper under the ground,
While radishes joke without a sound.
The harvest moon gives a gentle wink,
As veggies gather 'round to think.

A Symphony of Calm

In the quiet of the day, a gnome sneezed,
The trees all giggled, their branches seized.
A cat in sunglasses lounged by the brook,
While her fish friends plotted, taking a look.

Bubbles floated up, making puns on the way,
A turtle danced softly, caught in the sway.
Laughter twinkled as crickets played tunes,
Under the gaze of the grinning raccoons.

Foxes held court, sipping on mist,
Debating the best way to make toasts twist.
They hatched hilarious schemes with a cheer,
As the whispers rolled softly, crystal clear.

When night fell gently, the moon winked bright,
A frog croaked jokes under the silver light.
The calm, oh the laughs, made the world seem a game,
In this quiet delight, nothing was the same.

Unraveled Threads of Whispered Thoughts

A spider spun tales from her silken thread,
While a bat roamed low, checking under the bed.
The leaves snickered softly, exchanging a glance,
As a hedgehog in boots started a dance.

Whispers of dreams and mischief unfurled,
As squirrels debated their acorn world.
Puns flew freely with each gentle breeze,
While a bee in a bowtie took life with ease.

Under this chaos of communion and jest,
A wise old owl hooted, quite unimpressed.
'These thoughts are just threads from a comedy show,'
He chuckled in silence, 'Now watch the flow!'

With laughter entwined in the breath of the night,
Each creature saw joy in the flickering light.
As whispers unraveled, they twirled round and round,
Creating a symphony, oh what a sound!

The Depths of Solitary Reflection

In the pool of calm, a fish flipped around,
In search of a laugh, he found a lost sound.
He caught a reflection, then laughed at his face,
In this watery world, he found a new space.

Underneath the surface, where bubbles do roam,
A clam shared a joke, pointed out a foam.
As eels swam by, with a wink and a splash,
Together they formed a slippery bash.

Thoughts drifted gently on currents so wide,
A turtle swayed slowly, arms open wide.
'What's life without laughter?' he pondered and grinned,
At the depths of the silence where humor had sinned.

The ripples of laughter danced through the tide,
Crabs piled on top, wearing shells full of pride.
In reflections so vivid, a funny parade,
In the depths of the quiet, their joy never stayed.

Still Waters Reflecting Stars

Beneath the stars, where the frogs like to croak,
The pond turned into a mirror of smoke.
Ripples of giggles spread wide with the breeze,
While a raccoon in pajamas snatched up some cheese.

The moon gave a wink, with a glimmering spark,
As a firefly flickered, making its mark.
Jumpy reflections of bunnies at play,
Were losing their socks on this quirky display.

Calmness and laughter mingled quite free,
As owls debated the price of a tree.
While crickets conducted an orchestra bright,
The night sang a tune, a whimsical flight.

In the stillness profound, where humor takes root,
The stars shone down, giving a hoot.
In this dance of tranquility, all seemed just right,
With chuckles and whispers, they filled the night.

The Art of Unspoken Words

In a room full of chatter, I sip my tea,
Listening to silence, it sets me free.
My friends are all talking, their voices a race,
But I'm winning the battle, with silence and grace.

They ask me a question, I pause and I grin,
What's better than banter? A wink and a spin!
With silence as canvas, I paint with a shrug,
Art of unspoken words, it's like a warm hug.

When jokes hit their peak, I cool it right down,
A silent detective, no need for a frown.
While laughter erupts, I just sit there and beam,
In the realm of not speaking, I find my daydream.

The pause is electric, like popcorn on cue,
I stash my ambitions, who needs a hullabaloo?
With a wink and a chuckle, I say it's no crime,
To master the art of the pause every time.

Chorus of Serene Spaces

In the realm of the quiet, I twirl and I sway,
Each moment a note in an unplayed ballet.
With my cat on the sofa, we share the same space,
A duet of stillness, no need for a race.

The fridge hums a tune, a low melody,
While I ponder my snack—could it just be me?
A chorus composed of soft rustles and sighs,
We'll hold our grand concert beneath muted skies.

When my neighbor shouts loud, 'Turn down that noise!'
I giggle in silence, oh, the joys of poise!
For every raucous quip, I offer a grin,
In the symphony of quiet, where do we begin?

With tick-tock the clock plays its whimsical game,
Here silence is golden; it's not just a name.
Join me in laughter, but keep it discreet,
A chorus of serene, where the shy still can meet.

The Comfort in Stillness

Oh, the joys of just sitting, feet up on the chair,
Embracing the stillness, free from all care.
I take in the room with a sip of some tea,
The comfort of quiet, it's just you and me.

The dog takes a nap, dreams of chasing a bone,
While I share my thoughts with the dust on its throne.
In this cozy cocoon, we mingle, we rest,
In stillness, my senses feel utterly blessed.

The world rushes past, like a cartoon on speed,
But here's where I dwell, where I plant all my seeds.
With chuckles unspoken, a grin on my face,
I've mastered the art of a slow, gentle pace.

So let the clamor outside rattle the street,
I dance in the cozy, where silence feels sweet.
The comfort in stillness can't easily fade,
As I linger in laughter, blissfully arrayed.

Ripples in a Quiet Pond

A pebble drops softly, it circles and spins,
In the calm of the water, where silence begins.
Each ripple a giggle, a quirk of the night,
In the world of stillness, everything feels right.

Duck paddles by, with a nonchalant flair,
He quacks at the ripples, who could ever care?
The frogs look amazed, at this circus of fun,
In the quiet pond show, they bask in the sun.

The leaves whisper secrets, and trees sway along,
In a world painted playful, nature sings a soft song.
With laughter that's muted, yet colors so bright,
We dance on the edges, where day meets the night.

Every splash tells a story, yet hushes the noise,
I ponder my thoughts amidst nature's soft poise.
In ripples of laughter, my heart feels so light,
In a quiet pond's charm, everything feels right.

Emptiness as an Embrace

In a room with no sound, a chair laughs,
Dust bunnies hold court, discussing their paths.
The fridge hums a tune, off-key and loud,
It whispers secrets to the burgers, proud.

The toaster pops up with a grin so wide,
An empty mug winks, in coffee it hides.
When echoes dance around with a jig,
Even silence can get a bit too big.

A lonely cat yawns, strikes a bizarre pose,
While shadows play tag, wearing sunshine's clothes.
Each creak of the floor, a prankster at heart,
Turns quiet to chaos, a strange kind of art.

So here in this hush, where giggles reside,
Let's toast to the quiet, with sardines on the side.
In the absence of noise, we find laughter's threads,
As emptiness cuddles, with tickles instead.

Caress of the Soft Breeze

A gentle breeze sneaks through the window pane,
Chasing away papers, whispering their names.
It ruffles my hair like a mischievous friend,
And tickles my ears with the tales it sends.

The curtains dance wildly, like party-goers free,
As if they know secrets of what's yet to be.
The sun peeks around, with a wink and a grin,
Inviting the day for some chuckles within.

A bird breaks the mold, in a humorous flight,
Stumbling and tumbling, oh what a sight!
The leaves join the laughter, they flutter and twirl,
While I sit and chuckle, oh what a swirl.

So here's to the breeze, with its playful tease,
Turning mundane moments into such a breeze.
In the quietest corners, where giggles collide,
We find joy in the stillness, with laughter as our guide.

Fleeting Moments of Quiet

In the pause between breaths, a sneeze interrupts,
Bringing chaos to corners, or is it just blsub?
A moment of stillness, then boom—a loud clap,
As I search for my thoughts, they've taken a nap.

The phone buzzes softly, a cat meme appears,
I burst out in laughter, no hiding my cheers.
The clock ticks away like a spy with a grin,
Timing my chuckles, it knows how to spin.

A sock on the floor makes a dash for the door,
While my mind tries to sort out the tales of yore.
The shuffle of slippers echoes in jest,
As I ponder the meaning of humorous rest.

So let's savor the breaks, those short funny slips,
Where laughter can bubble like soda with fizz.
In the pockets of peace where joy like confetti,
Sprinkles our lives, whimsical and steady.

The Palette of the Unsaid

With colors unspoken, the silence takes flight,
A canvas awaits where shadows feel light.
The hues of the quiet can tickle the soul,
Creating a masterpiece that's funny and whole.

A wink from the colors, a nod from the shade,
Laughing at words that we never had made.
Splashes of joy dance on the empty space,
A chuckle erupts, what a curious chase!

The brush strokes of stillness, a comical spree,
Each stroke tells a story, oh how can this be?
The shades of the moment blend merrily so,
It's laughter in waiting, where whispers can flow.

In the gallery of silence, jesters hold court,
Painting our thoughts without needing a sport.
With each passing second, a vibrant surprise,
In the depth of the quiet, humor applies.

A Symphony of Silence

In a room so quiet, a cat gives a purr,
The sound of a sneeze makes the sofa stir.
Dust bunnies dance in a charming ballet,
While the clock ticks loudly, making time sway.

A mouse in the corner is caught in a stare,
With cheese on his mind, a feast laid with care.
The fridge takes a break, holding secrets so deep,
As we snicker at silence, pretending to sleep.

Outside the birds chirp, a mischievous tune,
But inside, we giggle like kids with a balloon.
The silence is thick, yet laughter does creep,
In this chaos of quiet, joy's ours to keep.

So here's to the moments we share without sound,
When muffled snorts echo; it's truly profound.
For in this wacky hush that we all can confess,
There's humor embedded in every less mess.

Embracing the Gentle Hush

In the still of the night, the fridge starts a hum,
While I talk to my shoelace, like it's some kind of chum.
Whispers of cats make me giggle for sure,
As they plot their next conquest, an unguarded drawer.

The pillows conspiring, they flip and they flop,
Each one taking turns to hold my loud pop.
The gentle hush wraps me like a soft blanket,
And I laugh at my snacks, the last ones I've banked it.

The chime of the clock always seems to be late,
Just like my attempts to seal my own fate.
In the laughter of quiet, secrets combine,
While I eat all the cookies and say they're divine.

So here in the stillness, I giggle and grin,
Finding humor in silence, let the funny begin.
For every loud moment, there's a time to be sly,
In this hush of our laughter, we'll always get by.

The Solace of Silence

In a world full of chatter, there lies a great perk,
Where not a word spoken isn't a quirk.
The dog blinks wisely, with no bark to share,
While I stare at my plants, pretending to care.

The wind starts to chuckle, brushing through leaves,
As my fish in the tank plots escape, if he believes.
I raise my eyebrow at the toaster in jest,
As it pops all the bread with a look so impressed.

The silence is buzzing with all kinds of thoughts,
Like why do my socks go on mismatched trot?
While my chair starts to creak at the stories it's told,
It's hard not to laugh at this calm, manifold.

So here's to the peace where the funny resides,
In this quietude gathering where humor abides.
Embracing the stillness where giggles can bloom,
I savor each moment — oh, how it can zoom!

A Canvas of Calm

A canvas so quiet, with colors subdued,
As my sneakers toe-tap to keep me amused.
The goldfish is grinning, or is that just me?
In this quietful madness, it's where I feel free.

The paint on the wall is drying too slow,
Like my brain in the morning, after a show.
Each gentle still moment, a joke to unfold,
Makes me laugh at my projects, so carefree and bold.

Butterflies flutter, without making a sound,
While I tiptoe through silence, my own luck I've found.
A whisper will echo, like a tickle of air,
And I giggle at shadows, that are hiding in there.

So here's to the calm, where funny can bloom,
Where sitting in silence feels just like a room.
With chuckles unspoken, and smiles on the wall,
In this quiet of joy, I find we have it all.

The Comfort of Quiet Corners

In a nook where whispers dance,
Lies a couch, a gentle chance.
Pillows piled up to the sky,
Dreams float past as time slips by.

Cats conspire, plotting schemes,
In their world of purring dreams.
With each nap, they claim their prize,
While I just smile and roll my eyes.

A dust mote flutters, taking flight,
In corners, there's a soft delight.
Crackers snap like mystery news,
Snack time whispers, no one snooze.

Laughter bubbles without a sound,
In the stillness, joy is found.
Come join the quiet, take a seat,
While on silence, we all feast.

A Haven of Gentle Murmurs

Amidst the buzz, I seek a hush,
Where every rush meets gentle blush.
Friends trade tales without a sound,
Their light is felt, but never found.

A teacup clinks, a secret shared,
In the bubble of calm, no one's scared.
Outside the chaos, I sit tight,
In the murmur, life feels right.

Socks mismatched, giggles abound,
Under blankets, warmth is found.
Laughter echoes, stays in space,
In this haven, we've found grace.

A cozy corner, soft as hugs,
Lurking cats with tiny shrugs.
In our kingdom, we're all queens,
Murmurs paint the air with dreams.

Ethereal Calmness in the Air

Breezes flutter through the trees,
As if they're sharing silly dreams.
Clouds doze off in a friendly line,
Whispers tickle like aged wine.

We tiptoe on the softest grass,
While squirrels gossip, full of sass.
Tension melts in soft sunlight,
Mirth dangles just out of sight.

Jellybeans and secrets shared,
Underneath the blossoms, dared.
Time winks brightly, plays along,
In comforts where we all belong.

So hush-coo with the rustling leaves,
Laugh with beauty that deceives.
For in this calm, let's not be shy,
Fun hides softly, just let it fly.

The Artistry of Silent Moments

Blank canvases of golden hue,
Await the brush of what we do.
Strokes of silence, colors blend,
Where laughter's silence never ends.

Fingers dance on unseen strings,
While my mind hums summer flings.
With every pause, absurdity blooms,
Quiet clarity shapes the rooms.

An awkward pause transforms the day,
As jokes float in a hushed ballet.
Chests swell up, our laughter we steal,
In silent moments, we burble and squeal.

Here's to the oddness, joyful and true,
With giggles that have no due.
The artistry in quiet schemes,
Turns silence into our grand dreams.

Echoes of Still Waters

In the pond where frogs just laze,
A fish sings tunes in silly ways.
The ripples dance and giggle loud,
While ducks parade, so proud, so proud!

The turtles laugh, they take a peek,
At soggy shoes of folks who sneak.
With every splash, a chuckle bursts,
In nature's jest, it sometimes thirsts.

The dragonflies play tag in flight,
Each zap and zoom a pure delight.
With every hum, a story spins,
Of wiggly worms and fishy fins.

But still the waters keep a grin,
Where silence sings, and jokes begin.
Life's quirky calm, so funny, bright,
In echoes soft, it takes its flight.

Wrapped in Nature's Silence

In woods where whispers softly tread,
The squirrels plot, while foxes spread.
A gentle breeze brings chuckles near,
As leaves conspire with silent cheer.

The bunnies boast of hidden snacks,
While owls roll eyes at funny quacks.
A twig snaps loud, a blanket breaks,
The laughter rolls, the silence shakes.

Each rustle holds a hidden jest,
Where critters share their finest best.
In shadows deep, with glee they pounce,
And nature's hush begins to bounce.

'Neath branches low, the giggles rise,
As treasures found become the prize.
Wrapped snug in giggles, soft yet sly,
The forest hums a lullaby.

The Lotus of Peace

In a pond where blooms appear,
The lotus waves away all fear.
It grins at frogs, a winking bloom,
With petals bright that chase the gloom.

The fish below do flip and splash,
While dragonflies engage in flash.
"Is that a dinner dance?" they say,
Nature's laugh keeps worries at bay.

A turtle nods, it's time to chill,
With jellybeans for every meal.
The lotus nudges, "Join the fun!"
"We've all got donuts, you'll be spun!"

In still waters, joy's not far,
Where peace and giggles softly spar.
The blooms will tell you, sweet and bright,
Life's just a joke wrapped up in light.

Hibernation of Forgotten Voices

In the woods, the whispers nap,
Beneath the snow, they take a lap.
The owls and bats, they crack a jest,
While sleepy bears put jokes to rest.

The trees trade tales of winter's bite,
As critters hibernate for light.
With snuggled dreams in cozy dens,
They plot their fun for warmer 'gins.

A frosty breeze brings chuckles low,
As snowflakes dance like comedy's flow.
Each muffled sound, a soft reprise,
In winter's blank, the laughter lies.

When spring arrives, they'll spill their beans,
And wake the world with playful scenes.
For now, the hush is quite divine,
In silence thick, they wait and dine.

Sheltered in Gentle Shadows

Underneath the leafy bow,
A squirrel whispers, "Wow, wow!"
Watching grasshoppers dance,
In their leafy, green romance.

Ants march in a crazy line,
Not a single one can dine.
They trip and tumble with delight,
In their silent, silly flight.

Gnomes giggle in the sun,
While pondering who's the fun one.
A breeze teases a fern,
Making it twist and turn.

The world is quiet, can't you see?
Even the cat pretends to flee.
In laughter's soft embrace we hide,
Amid gentle shadows, side by side.

Soft Shadows of Unspoken Words

Whispers float like little kites,
In the warmth of mellow nights.
Bunny ears perk up with grace,
As they join the silent race.

Cacti giggle in the sun,
They're no chefs, but still have fun.
Needles poke with crafty glee,
As soft shadows tease the bee.

Mice cover their tiny ears,
While the owl lands with no fears.
"Keep it down!" the flowers shout,
As the wind twirls all about.

Underneath the starlit glow,
The laughter weaves soft and slow.
In a garden where words flee,
It's the quiet that sets us free.

The Serenity Found Between Heartbeats

Tick-tock goes the clock so round,
In the silence, giggles abound.
Tickled by a mischievous breeze,
Snickering through the tallest trees.

In the middle of a quiet jig,
A worm shows off its little wig.
Hopscotch dreams in muted hues,
Bouncing in invisible shoes.

Daffodils nod their sleepy heads,
As the moon hums to the threads.
Caterpillars hold a debate,
On who gets the last cupcake plate.

Each heartbeat, a soft embrace,
In this laughter, we find our place.
With each pause and every sigh,
We twirl in the twilight, oh so spry.

An Oasis of Quietude

In the garden, whispers play,
A frog croaks, "Hip-hip-hooray!"
Balloons float without a sound,
While shadows gather all around.

Hedgehogs share their secret tales,
Of adventures by the gales.
Without a noise, they roam and laugh,
As they nibble on the grass.

The turtles take a slow, deep breath,
Living life as if no stress.
In stillness, they find their groove,
Ignoring all but just to move.

In this land of silent cheer,
Come closer, lend me your ear.
For in this stillness, there's a spark,
Where laughter dances in the dark.

Navigating the Silent Abyss

In the depths where whispers twirl,
Even crickets give a gentle whirl.
Puddles of quiet with laughs to share,
As socks go missing without a care.

Bubbles burst in the void so wide,
An echo sings where the silly hide.
With every footstep, silence squeaks,
A game of tag, no one peeks.

Joyful giggles float like air,
Where even shadows pause to stare.
The carpet's soft, a blue-gray sea,
Who knew peace could be so free?

Yet in this realm of muted cheer,
The cat thinks silence is a frontier.
He pounces on dust without a sound,
In this quiet place, he's tightly wound.

Threads of Tranquility

A gentle hum wraps around the day,
While sneaky squirrels hunt for play.
With mischief wrapped in cozy seams,
Tranquil threads weave wild daydreams.

Rabbits frolic in quiet glee,
While the goldfish giggle under the sea.
A fabric of laughter softly glows,
Threaded in silence where no one knows.

Tangled yarn sprawls by the door,
A dance of chaos, we all adore.
A sneeze brings giggles to the fray,
Where even peace can't find its way.

Slumbering shadows wiggle around,
In threads of laughter, joy is found.
With every stitch, a giggle swells,
In this realm where silence tells.

The Calm Before the Breath

A hiccup dances through the still,
As turtles plot their next great thrill.
Breathless moments filled with glee,
Oh! Who knew calm could be so zesty?

A monk's chant breaks, then starts to laugh,
While a butterfly sketches a comic staff.
In the stillness, comic strips delight,
As every laugh takes graceful flight.

The universe pauses, holding tight,
To the bubbling joy before the night.
Paper boats on ponds do sail,
In this quiet, where giggles prevail.

Yet caution creeps in with silly doubt,
That perhaps calm is not as stout.
The moment swells, then bursts with cheer,
And lays a warm, tranquil sphere.

Peace Found in Petals

Beneath blossoms, shadows sway,
Buzzing bees join the bouquet.
With every petal gently twirled,
A buffet of laughter softly unfurled.

Chasing daisies through the breeze,
While ants play tag among the leaves.
Each flower holds a tale so funny,
In this silence, there's no hurry, honey!

Tulips giggle, and roses wink,
While sleepy snores disrupt the link.
Butterflies flutter, mock the calm,
In this petal party, chaos a balm.

Silence hums, a zany tune,
As nature croons beneath the moon.
In every bloom, a joke resides,
Peace found in petals, where joy abides.

www.ingramcontent.com/pod-product-compliance
Lightning Source LLC
Chambersburg PA
CBHW070304120526
44590CB00017B/2557